In every erotic encounter there is an invisible

and ever-active participant: imagination, desire.

Eroticism is first and foremost

a thirst for otherness.

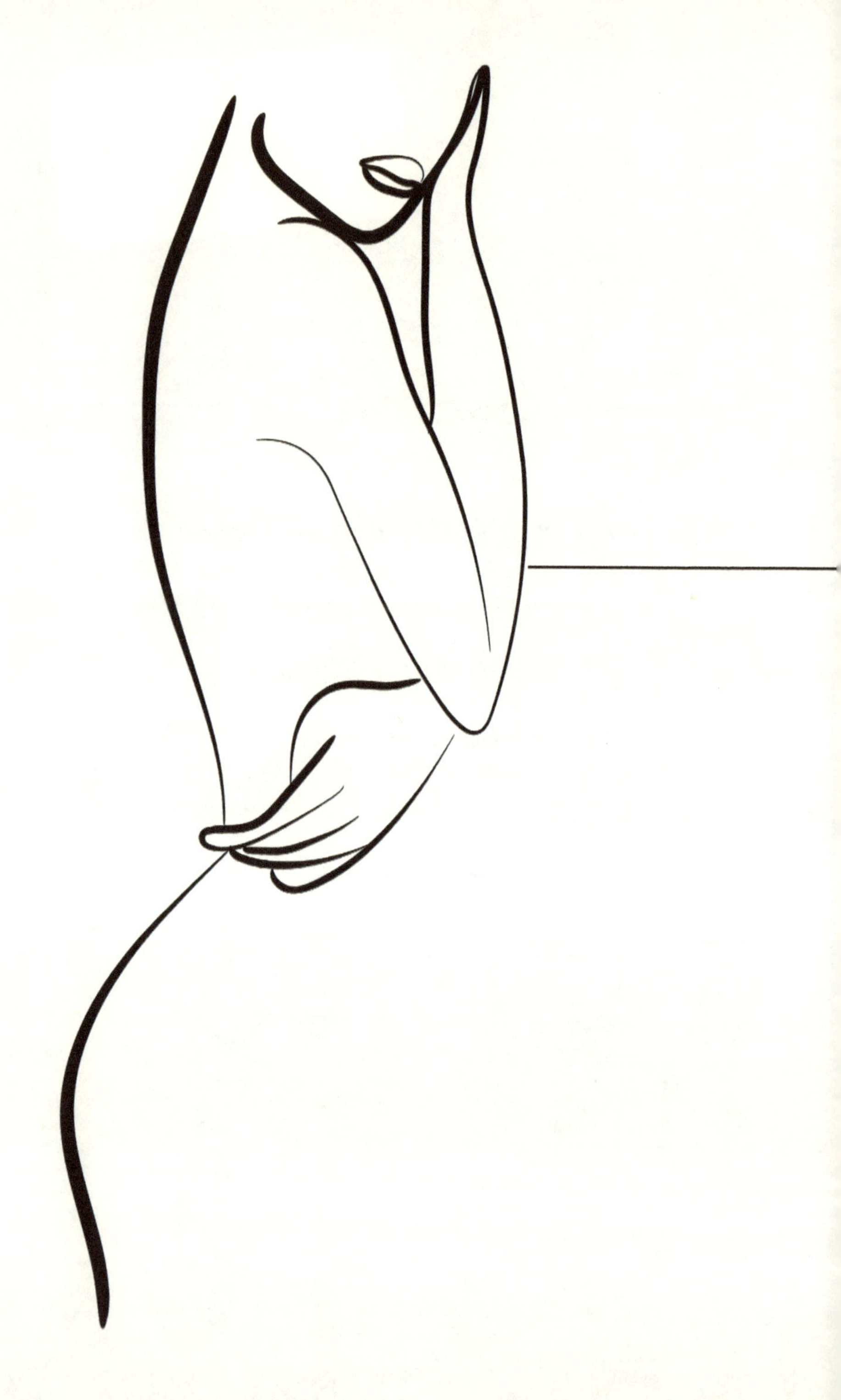

EROS
unleashed

KANCHAN
BHATTACHARYA

CREDITS :
Art and Edit : Sonali Rasal
Book Layout & Design: ILANOS STUDIOS 9422517939
Publication House: NOTION PRESS

COPYRIGHT

DISCLAIMER
This book is entirely based on the poet's imagination
and his relationship with 'The Muse'. The poet and
the publishing house have undertaken all reasonable
and prudent efforts to ensure that the sentiments of any
person, country or community are not deliberately hurt.

Price: Rs 220 / $8 plus postage $3

"To my friend, Shehnaz - Seven Years"

Dear Reader

Poetry is plucking at the heartstrings, and making music with them. ~ Dennis Gabor

Do you think nomads have a religion, or like me, you need to be a faithless one, whose books speak the poetry of wayward love?

To me, a poet's work, poetry, is the collection of fragments of a novel waiting to be written. Random words, fleeting view, romantic words, naked trysts, meetings and seances, déjà vu, the id of a solo traveller in Fantasia talking to his cooked up women, themselves in highs of ecstasy.

Poetry is about tenderness too. Imagine the sunset, black sands of a nowhere beach, and hear her say don't touch me more, or touch me with you finger of fire..

Cafuné - The act of caressing or tenderly running fingers through a loved one's hair

Cafuné
Breathing vapour
Fragrance of an affair
An upturned face

Eros will take you on the journey of the subconscious, read into the world of yesterdays, the unspoken, unseen, undone Odeyssies of poetry, the nomad within me.

~ Kanchan Bhattacharya

CONTENTS:

UNDONE

Unspoken

Love is an attempt to penetrate another being,
but it can only be realized if the surrender is mutual.

~ Octavio Paz
The Labyrinth of Solitude
and Other Writings

Prelude

nouns, spring yields, flowers sprouting from grass, incidentals amid the cobblestones, lodgements, board, breakfast, and privileges, throwbacks to the times of threads, towing kites through fist holds, and casual thoughts- dew and dust

verbs, bougainvillea waving long arms with a thousand petals and safe houses built in arbours, bamboo arches tied with secrets kisses, cigarettes shared with caresses of needs and words spoken not often, rare, sparse longings again seeking to undress and make love in distances less than atoms and molecules melting only like stalagmites, drop by drop - slowly, seeking lips of stalagmites

pauses, sentience breathing hard, short of breath, sounds, diphthongs, short phrases, echoing in caves...

As the owner of a sinful heart, I speak now with longings deeper than the deepest of dark lust. You can see my eyes, the fiery inferno. Summer of blue, zephyrs walk through corridors; her eyes wait for southern monsoons.

At summer times of long ago, I admired, the gods and goddesses of Rome and Greece, immersed myself in an ocean of imaginations. Now my goddesses have names, and they speak and write.

kanchan bhattacharya

Of late, the hand that tried touching you changed to red, because touches tell tell-tales of how often I have found pleasures in touching joys alone, for myself, her and just that.

Though the other one I touched changed too, the connection was electric. It lasts in me, and in her for it is like a quarter year liaison, a time of faraway summers, and the times I have to go home in the monsoon rains thinking of you, and then face the fall in Autumn, lonely leaves falling, and the long Winter, the Spring...

It is hard to stay under cover. The burial of secrets often is for ever, nothing remains, except the dream of that once, and the reality of the now, stuck with the pain and sorrow because it cannot be relived, unless I walk out of comforts.

It is a poem, isn't it, that all songs last for the moment, the music remembered, but not heard, unless my red hand returns to cheat, once, twice and always when there is a chance...

I have to say many things. I have been naked with her with thoughts under cover at home too. It was her, a lover, in repose in my mind. I feel her flesh with my mind's touch, it is electric, a contact of stimulus, this infidelity...

Yes, I touched that adrenaline wired to my soul.

Old men have the tendency to create statues of love. A full-blown woman with a sweet face. Perhaps with a hint of tragedy in her past.

She is 40, he, two decades older. He thinks of a waterfall. Of Ophelia afloat in a dream pond, alive and playful in her madness. He stares at a dusty guitar on a stand, waiting for his fingers, the boom of flamenco chords.

His room has a French window. His room is Reality. The window links him to the surreal world of love. He imagines he has found love- his room tethers him to his wants. He thinks aloud to himself... "You are my French Window".

A smile paints itself on the window. Then the lips become a face. The face becomes a woman, who pirouettes and melts into invisibility. In epilogue, Always a full lip, and caressing eyes. She is now 50, he two decade older.

It is beautiful to be in love, never to tell.

Ensemble

Tapestry of time
Woven on lost memories,
White silken mosaic...

An ensemble of caresses in the mosaic of Time, little lusty rain drops lingering on tendrils, lovers slipping their fingers into each other's, clinging to the lee beneath the ivy. The sky is a canvas load of black and white, and sometimes just a show of raving streaks of light...

Nights do not whisper
They pour deep dark loneliness
Disconsolate tears...

A Day Begins

This stream of blood, love in a summer's breaking dawn;
a last tango; a late night...

Sleep never returned to our eyes. Molten promises; a red
flow, alive like lies, and dead like cold touches of ice.

You never promise but enchant; lisping kisses, you
begin infernos- like a chameleon merged with the night's
darkness; paused, eternal in wait. Love menstruates;
death calls. Not this time; a train roars by- periodical,
red. Nearby, willows sway, monsoons touch; vernal
summer, glimpses of naked leaf ; desire. This stream;
tamarind, microscopic memorized, breathing, impulses.

Aspirate, face to face, in a forest home, folded over each
other, not letting go. In the warm perma-frost, in wistful
hope, gazelles halt in mid-stride; in the wilderness, a
frenzied heap of sighs folds into melodies of rushing
blood...

Summer moments, heat
A dust storm ahead, a tryst
Semibreve, restive

The first coherent thought of the day streak through
drawn curtains. We stare at the roof, spent, disentangling,
melting, becoming human, detached, distant, real, islands
in distinct oceans, faraway planets.

　　　kanchan bhattacharya

Ink streaks, lingering unfolding new stories, dark, grey ashen red.

My long vigil over, the last thought before I slept gazing at her face... Beautiful!

Raindrop sequences listless thoughts; street sounds at play with piano notes, two kisses in a dream, of Ophelia

I make up too many things, even you. I am now editing my memories, but that never changes. Time is a tetrahedral crystal, a nascent diamond. This madness is meteoric.

Serpent and Piscean, she, the mermaid, had a name.

But I am trying to forget how it all began. We closed a door behind us, and now, we are inside, afloat in the shadow zone. Lemons and whispers, undoing each other's shyness in shallow breaths.

I still wish to be an island; where the sea sleeps when wild storms arrive; I wish you love, whispers say on tranquil silver sand shores.

White flowers, and her hair, afloat in a placid pool. Somewhere there was a fire. Madness is a phase...

Never Say

I chose to be the voiceless insider, a drunken lover telling stories to the shadow walking along on stilts. A gallery of beautiful but forgotten images afloat in nether oceans, a cup of hemlock, a spoonful of the asp's venom.

Still remembering the bare talons of daring abandonment, whispers roaring in fiery proximity, in this opium walk. Smiles of innocence draping that raging feral desire, rhythms, surges, spasms of ecstasy on a catwalk.

I still love you, dear Illusion, to mirages- I remain drawn, through sunset days, dark nights, twilight and naked dawn, making love to gypsy fractals...

I am holding your hands, shadow woman, on a tryst beneath the August starlight. It is a rock, that burden of shyness, reticence, defeat.

Never say the short sentence, the three words of finality.

Wanna be thoughts, dark
A drunken poet meanders, lost
She had closed her heart.

Never mind, midnight has stories, a few who, calcified, know the details, the minutiae untold; the heartburns in the wings on stage, the curtains in velvet… How else do you and I part?

No dream lasts enough, even the orgasm, ephemeral, secret and too personal. If I love you, you do too. Never ask. It rained then, as you shivered, became the dust in the mural; timeless because the cabbie knocked, we parted and stared.

Lovers cheat, don't they? But the night does too, tomorrow stays in my heart, and it has a name.

Yours…

Wanton, these wants, needs
January, chrysanthemums
Hide old love stories

I have always consoled you. Dreams come and go. Sometimes, when the floods come, dreams die. Within the mask of monsoon, I lie awake through the rain, to hear rain drops on windowsills asking me to feel your breath, to watch your soft breasts that rise and fall, in the stray lights of our thundering skies, and stop.

Your whispers merge with love, traced in white dynamite streaks. All my poems try to intrude. Running with the wind, I recite my broken words to my footfalls.

I am obsessed like a river in spate- tumbling sand. Longings sans reason stir the quiet night; obsessed cyclones begin rituals of intrusive intimacy; monsoon brings thought of grey hues.

Labyrinthine thoughts... When then can we begin to close in on each other?

To be, not to be, whispering to ourselves, this murmuring of rain.

To never say we love, to never say we dream, to never say we shall part. It is the rain keeping us awake, as we lie cradling unspoken poems. Inconsequential words, images, read, unread in flames, unquenched, un-kissed thoughts linger, winter's caresses, swarming magical fruit, this.

Good nights at dawns, inspiration sleeps between two writers, between lovers, nothing but yearnings.

I can never say it, nor can she. We have taboos, for our love is as sweet as the crime, adults soaked in adultery.

Midnight

Tactile verse in messy hunger, nimble fingers weaving plaits of traces, pleasure paths twisting jasmine fragrance. In a room with mirror walls and infinite images of lust, impatience begins sounds of music, breathing...

The night has killed itself, no questions asked, arrhythmia, an alien sylph, invades, poetry rains from a lover's soft breasts, erotic, yet cursed. I shuffle two clouds in a wild midnight romance...

Ashes arrive with sunlight.

My Unsold Painting

Walking on sand, I shed my inhibitions, I stare at the footprints of a woman walking before me, as she walks on my poems, steps on each word, on erotic wily whispers that fled from her.

I draw apart the curtains, and insert a mean alliterated sequence to titillate, to persuade her, like how a woman seeks company, some smoky dreamer making love behind the red curtains, drunk with rum, to make her breast stiff and waiting, with her legs spread, naked, and saying come on.

You eat this, she says, and shows her aroused goose fleshed breasts, (oh not that again!) She says she serves sex, sympathy, some tea, and Playboy pictures of a century ago, and heaves a sigh, and says, put your signature with the ink of saliva, your tongue for a pen.

A reverie, promises, poems. An anytime sex machine, a robot, she never likes poems. It, I mean she, waits in a corner of the room, connected to the ethernet, to power-lines with wires. Then I ask her, if she is ready, and she says yes, lubricated, pulsing and she walks to my bed, promising to read any poem that I write, and to recite those anywhere, anytime, any day, any night.

Now you know why my poems, though lucid, exclude me, exclude you. They are not meant for you, they shall remain on a page of dreams, abstract passionate longings for a dream body, a brand name with a tattoo. Just mind-speak, hoping for telepathy.

     kanchan bhattacharya

You are my first love. We never did it. I drew you nude, helpless, on an easel in my youth, from the imaginative emptiness of dawning adolescence, and I am carrying you to my death.

Of the poet's mind, of his dead flesh, little poems brew in the moonshine left in his half empty tumbler. Little images, waves, and tides merge with the rhythm of words…

In limbo hang thoughts tourmaline crystals in caves dance in darkness. Tactile bliss, fingers write music, scarlet traces upon wily lips, her breasts hold my eyes. Quintessential, sine qua non of my existence. How little we know of erotic ties; symbols celebrate this lust. Lingering raindrops begin their coaxing on the poet's mind. His Muse lies naked on a bed, listening to the low staccato notes from the poet's keyboard, as he types erotic thoughts.

This is not a moment that stands still in time. He dreams of volcanoes, the areolas of the Earth that spew lava. His woman dreams of his soft voice. Two dreams cross each other, unaware. Tendrils clasp emptiness, and ivies climb trellises of tragic tremolos, voices echoing questions of each other, are you here?

A sleepless sentinel, the owl peers at the prodigal miscreant, a drunken poem that walks upon the dotted white line in the middle of the street.

A long walk-in loneliness, this summer tempts, penciled lines slither, doodles imitate intimacy.

3 AM Rhymes

Marooned in a marriage with silence, midnight is a long wake, watching thoughts begin the dance of Autumn swirls. We hear the tranced breathing of a muted gazelle, a poem paused amid iambs, swollen like I do, I do not go on in your caresses. A lonely sound comes from high in the sky, as an unknown flight traverses my dream space, and then I hear the first drop of rain.

Touch me not, my love
The pitter and the patter
Of ice cold droplets

Silent words of the heathen, come hither kind, into my mind come the whispers, do you have Time? Iambs and meter walk on stiletto heels, tip tapping on in an echoing corridor on a chequered chess-board of black and white tiles, and try to merge with the dark haze at the far end.

Stand still, lost voices
Falling leaves, a rustler steals
Old diary entries

Once again, it was like yester night, twilight hours, and solitude. Welcome, 3 am...

Lonely aeroplane
From Mumbai to Kolkata
White streak over me

To myself, whispers to keep, buried deep from episodes and trysts, summer stories, adrift in the breeze, little touches of love still rippling in my heart... To myself I write the music of a night, the longing of a faraway day, the lyrics of a dream, the Sundays in the park watching the birds... To myself, empty memories returning in my sleep...

Astir in Neverland blues, I greet the dawn of strange hues, black in the Nadir of the West, grey in the Zenith where I walk, and the tinge of red ahead, rubbing my eyes, I feel the moist earth, the intangible presence of the unknown day to be, the silence within pulsing in the rhythm of Time.

When the night dies upon me: when all whispers cease; when poems hide in the mist, and loneliness itself becomes the mist, I dream a little of the wisps that hide everything about you, I wait for the moonlight to talk to me...

To myself then, in loneliness bequeathed...

Skin and More: To A Lover

Love was there in my kisses upon your skin, and my saliva left my genes within. I left my marks all over you, you see that parchment carried an autobiography, a meandering long trail of moaning phonemes, the confessions of sultry nights, and dreams.

Telltales arrive in cavalcades of pages whispering of memories astir in insolent monsoon winds. The wilderness, in strange winding lanes with journeys, promises, waking up sexed, insane. We have lied- there is no truth to unfold, strangers to those who left us in the cold.

This was Paradise. This was from where we fell. We synchronized wings, as only time can tell if those DNA imprints on motel bed sheets would claim us finally, mark the subtle deeds- quanta of love tattooed in frenetic probes between naked bodies, soul to soul, closed.

There are brazen tell tales, marks, stories- passages upon the highways and high seas where names carved on stones and trees and our passports stamped, never cease. Someday, when we are gone, they may claim history in strange rooms was written, aflame.

Truant runaways from life's vaudeville shows- astir, gasping, sweating, and aglow as the eons pass by, parchments arrive on Time's door. This skin has stories to tell, and more!

Venus lives in this inferno. One by one the pages burned; smoke came from faded kisses falling into the fire that danced with dazzling orange hues. She sat contemplating at the end of whatever was left to burn in her heart or in what was once love.

Doors slowly closed, turning the quotient of existence into null and the rest became a river of glacial passion, frozen stories riding into eternity on moraine.

Coming back to her, he watched the embers of yesterday and a violin curling into deathly sleep, its bow still rubbing strings making tuneless love, and songs became screams.

She threw it all, chestnuts crackles hung in the fire of reminiscences- burn, burn, recall none, paper like changing colours- sepia, brown, black then to ashes floating in air, a shadow tiptoeing along flickering amber fingers reaching the sky.

Every day, she remembers nudity and the clothes of touch. She stands by the windows of pain, ironing all those folds of intimacy that came with the flow of life, impulses and stokes of a wanton tongue trying to speak in languages of twosomes hidden inside closets, tipped over by the deeds of arson in merry abandon...

lost forbidden thoughts
milling images, desire
stranded forever

Hunger in Northern Lights

Devour me, she asked, a piece of chewing gum unashamedly swallowing her lips painted in rouge, between pauses of manicuring her enameled tips. The parlor was her body and a white tiled dream, her boudoir. She had dark eyelashes, and flakes of mica afloat in a bowl of time, between the curls was a comb, clinging to that nothing tint of her skin.

In my arms in that bougainvillea arbor was red satin, wrapped around the torso of a poem that spoke to me again, and said, hear me sing my sighs and the nestling night fluttered a little, squirming and wriggling with the Moon and dark clouds...

The dream recurs with a young love, distanced in time, with a glass wall and hope eternal, in a sibilant whisper, "devour me", she said, "till I die, bereft of every word in my mind. Take me home, into your books painted in red like a bride, and my dark deep whispers clothing every moment in memories that never be, in a trousseau"...

Don't ask me if I love you. You know the answer, in the flashing of Northern lights hanging in never ending cold nights. I am hungry, still hungry, waiting to hear you say softly, devour me...

Meter in Love? ..Yes!

Sometimes….

There was a dynamic throb of unknowns invading gently when we were in our teens, it wasn't unusual to wait for twenty odd rings before we picked up the phone, the villain in our hearts in sync. We never knew the joys that a pair of bell sounds mixed with pauses- ring-ring, wait, ring-ring, ring-ring… could do. A teenage sister would grin- boy, your girl, can she sing, she would ask… teasing trying to listen to the caller's voice.

Meter, arrythmia, and the wonders of a rogue heart, the joys of walks in parks, and that solace in lonely places, hunting for dreams. Soul and soul mate. Mister Yin meets Miss Yang.

Anapests. Words that rhyme, and then not. Love has meter like tiptoes walking in ballets. Heady with anoxia and beats of timpani, beatboxing, waits forever, testimonials to stolen kisses, runaways. Yes rhythms. And fibrillation, asynchronous tell-tells, blushes, trespasses.

Shell shocked with mailed words in an inbox in those Morse code days, ticket tapes, teenagers in their sixties, women in sweet fifties, sixties. They run between trysts and time, humming tipsy tremolos, harmonica yodeling and solos.

Does love have a meter? Did you not know how the wind chimes on summer days, the rolls, and the wild waves…

        kanchan bhattacharya

Love is. Sometimes, sometimes.

Sometimes. Drunken nights memorized when rain does-teases, taunts, kisses, mesmerizes with its iambs and pentameter, verse and wanton verse, poised on the edges, invasions, inversed trails, raindrops. Tartars, Turks, Saracens, the Huns, swords raised, Crusades. Criss crossing reflections of waves rippling in a pool on the street, streetlamps. Rage. Pieces of paper, torn passages, starved. Her tears, droplets, and her timid yes. Yes, yes, yes.

Eros. The meter. Feet and beat. Love, live, alive, tapping beat, rhythmic feet, poems roses, minstrels coarse, risqué, but touches, intimate, close. Puckered red lips…

Iambs, trochee. Guarded spondee, twisting anapest. Visitors in the starkness of wanton muses. Stirrups and gallops. Whispers stopped, stares of lust.

Pitter patter, glass panes, rain, lanes, spiders, curtains drawn, locked, sinus rhythm, insane, stiletto heels, echoes.

And yes, you know this prowling mind in twilight hours past midnight, flickering, evanescent neon signs saying adios from aisles of dance halls. Closed doors.

Sometimes, sometimes, sometimes, sometimes. Love has its own meter- yes. Always!

She enters my studio apartment, on pretexts. In sealed little cardboard boxes, she returns sugar, loaned, laced with purloined love.

She stands with her dreams, home grown red strawberries. Bonsai trees flower in the garden on my table, they remind me of a captive spring.

This has a name. In an envelope, lie my kisses, colorless, dry. Once again, I find on the other side imprints of lipstick from her lips and her whispers.

She never told me she likes chocolates smeared on her breasts. Anticipation brings tremors, she once left me a touch emailed when she bathed…

Stained glass brings colors in a kaleidoscope of twisted desire. The doorbell chimes again.

Ivy caresses, her
Intrusions, tendrils, flowers
Bring hennaed whispers…

          kanchan bhattacharya

Soft whispers, sunsets tied to her dark eyes. Pages rustle, words become serpents. I wait for that mouthless kiss of soul felt desire. In a halfway house, I imagine her neck, then the curved back//feline//electric poetess... Muse

Alive so often
Phoenix. Labyrinthine maze
So often she dies…

She is poised in a time lapse recess. The sun is blanked out- sunbeams have become stars. In this empty homeland, I am the native, she, the alien invader.

Down memory lane
Inevitably listless
Flames; napalm scars, burns…

Unvoiced, in this silence comes a thought-

We. A new feeling
Rife with hope and swift denials
A new game. Eros

This is ellipsis, the black dot of the beginning, the continuum of pain, as I climb a rock face, groping for handholds, pitons rammed into cleaves between night and dawn, and I woke to silence in a dead cocoon of meanings between two bodies distanced for want of rhyme…

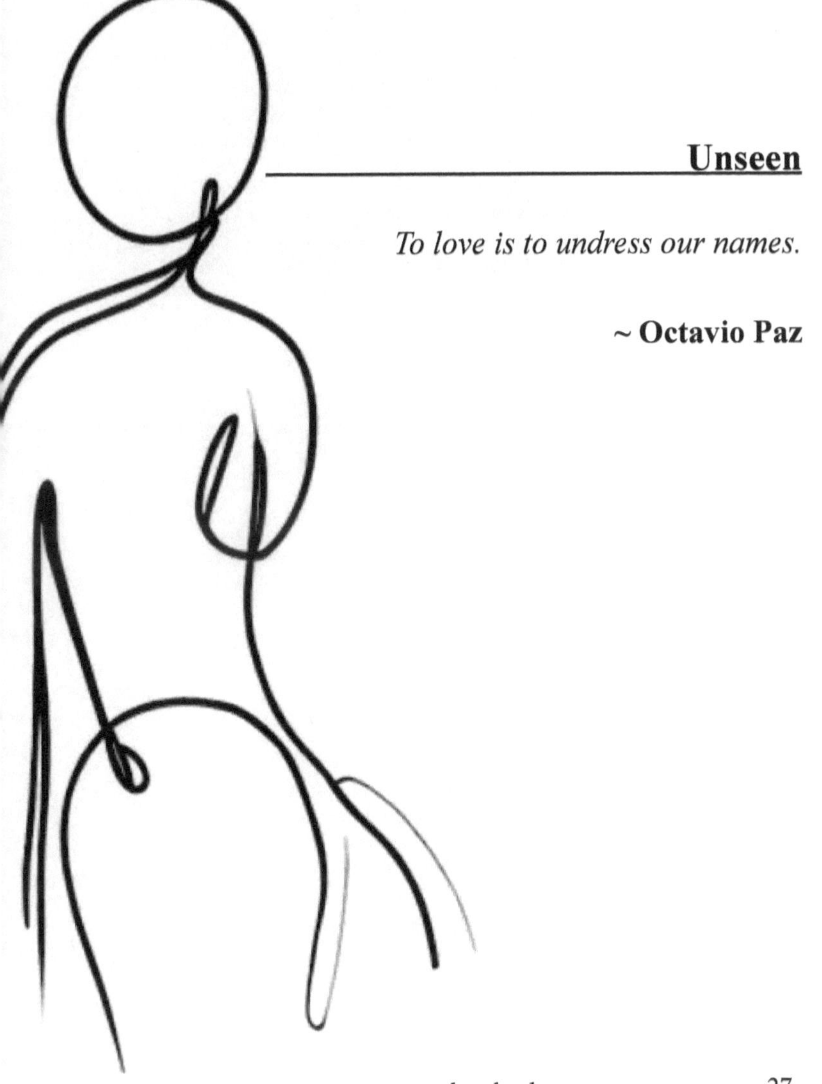

<u>Unseen</u>

To love is to undress our names.

~ Octavio Paz

kanchan bhattacharya

Twilight Tryst

Let me see you, Verse.

(... abseiling on a rope tethered to pitons tapped into the cracks in the rocks, along an eagle's nest above the trees. I am alone, resting on a ledge, secure but wishing to fall into the river, a thousand feet below. I let go, leap, swing, and land on the ledge, sixty feet down, breathing still, breathing easy...)

Are you traversing my soul, in the meter of a two beat prelude tied in pause and throb, throb and pause, and then trying a game of silhouettes and shadows, the mist and cloud breaching an open window, cold and rife with whispers dancing in a derelict tremolo, a tango in slow time?

Let me see you, Poem. You stole in, slept wrapping me with stories of amour only to be lost in the dunes of a desert, forlorn like a Bedouin trying to find an oasis hidden in a faraway mirage...

Let me see you, Impatience. You, visitor to my eyes drooping with longings for sleep, in a transit, anonymity afloat in blank pages and sketches of charcoal dreams, shapes unknown, humming tipsy words, merging with the quiescence of soft dancing Aurora Borealis sheets in the North skies, shimmering refractions and reflections, myth and magic, all said and done, playing truant with Hypnos, Nymph of Ado...

I knew you, Insomnia when you say
hush. Your fingers walk along my neck,
tap Spring. You write your words like
every night does- nude, naked, bare.

You said it so softly, calling out to me,
Eros...

     kanchan bhattacharya

Falcon

This monsoon has moods. A primordial deluge, this mad rain, a waterfall from the skies. An angina settles in a dark patched dream of torn sails, of a ship lost at sea. If once I let you in, my thoughts, now gentle, would change into wayward strays, the ingress surprises.

A wet falcon settles on my outstretched palms. The rain murmurs into my ears. Feel me, touch me, take me, you say. The falcon becomes an idol of desire, impatient as the moments pass.

Narcosis begins with the rhyme of pitter patter raindrops. I try to sleep. You sleepwalked into my dreams.

a paintbrush dipped in the dark ink of whispers and purple lips with blackberry stained kisses, in a faraway summer of intimacy, wistful straddled bodies tangled in sheets, nestling faces, proximal hair, an aroma, deft strokes of calligraphy in words chosen in the language the muse offers...

the music of rain, murals on a wall of silent desire, slithering images on a canvas of glass, poetry begins, once again the rhythms of breathing, the rhymes of monikers, the crescendo of arrivals, letting go in uninhibited surrenders...

whisper my favourite words, for you are taken forever...

A Thimbleful

She was hurt, but she was not because she was watching herself cleansing her toes with soap and water. She was watching a girl, herself, from another time, tending to her wounds in secret, wiping the blood that was oozing and dripping drop by drop into the sheet beneath her.

She was hurt, but she pretended she was not. She ruffled the pages of a beauty magazine, scrutinizing images. Women- round and soft, smiling, unreal postures staring back at the camera, and she was the camerawoman, into her eyes, even as she was bleeding from her wounds, many mouths created by brutal men now laughing outside the doors, each guffaw adding to her pain. She closed herself, wishing away those raucous sounds.

Somnambulant footsteps told the story one more time at dusk, even when the only word in her body was no, no. The colors of scarlet oozes, and her recoiling in futility against memory of the invader, the insane reality, touches of beasts, fangs biting into her...

The vocabulary of violent pains, the nouns of hurts and the present continuous verbs of insanity. And soon there was night...

Metamorphosis

How often have you seen a mirage in the darkness of a starless night? I have tried to wish it away, to fold it neatly in the layers of a dream, to be seen and then forgotten, to be felt and yearned for in the morning after.

And how often have I tried to ask you, to set your palms upon mine, and to look into my eyes?

In a could be world
We would kiss; in a real one
Wanton clouds would rain

A grain of wet sand, a feather and a whisper; magical words in a monsoon night, in a ceaseless poem; a long gasp as imagination stalks a long memorized shadow morphing into a torso.

It is the silence
That hangs behind drapes of lust
Seduced in solace

And now, I ask, are you ready?

Ode to Eros at Dawn

Candles still whisper in the wind; they moan before they gasp and let out the last wisps unseen. Her kisses remain etched on memories; yet nothing remains the same...

Amorous twilight
Dawn still far away, delayed
An untimely rain...

A kerosene lantern flickers and beckons poems; a woman awakens to her man's arousal; languor and consent contrive a duet, a symphony of timeless moves, each ends in a crescendo of unspoken practiced endearments.

As the monochromatic night bows out from this strange censored yet enchanted room, they escape into silver lined clouds, grey skies awaiting sunrises, promises, enticed by Eros, a candid surrender in a facile, tender, gentle desert; an oasis, an erotic zone of kisses, like mushrooms in full bloom, whispered wants.

Astir amid rain
Allured, inebriated lust
Serpent of Eden...

kanchan bhattacharya

Stranded, because yesterday was a chase, from dawn to last light, a flight into the night, and today would a day, chasing tomorrow.

Ah, here comes today, wagging its tail. A new story, sunlit. No clouds, no rain, miles of road, a few lines of thought then...

This darkness, this mist
Time hides its secrets; she hides-
Her desire no less

As the road unfolds amid tulip fields, a dotted white line marks the approach to the jetty beyond the curves.

The ferry called "consent" sounds its foghorn, still invisible in the mists of dawn.

She was the breeze that passed through my fingers, invisible, synchronized with mirages of wild lusty breasts, of hungry concave hollow hordes of carnivorous dreams, and yes, thoughts that sang in wordless forays into the mind through the ether between us.

I am the magician, caught in a word trap, alone on a sand dune, exiled by a disarrayed spell. I am sad, because all the magic I know does not work in this quantum space. I am thirsty, yet the oasis remains far away, it recedes into sunsets.

This is love on a page unknown, an open journey, no destination to reach. We are new here, growing into the chrysalis, a dream not yet formed.

We have chosen to be; I am, she is, but the planes of existence have not anchored yet. There is light, and there is the breeze. A little mad, a little of all that could be, but not quite that which I wish...

Braille et al

Braille, incomplete text
Midnight's messages, endless
Poems sans caresses

This you are, a raging storm in quiescence, a whispering
tornado in my dream...

Need I say more, I listen to the breeze in Spring mornings,
to the poems in the painting.

And then you are the rain that happened in the sky of
dark deep stirrings...

The Moon and Seasons

We built an affair in shallow crescent moons in West skies, an empire of impulses reaching out from sunsets to sunrises. The moon grew every day.

Summer sunshine
Coconut beaches; waves
Rippling seashore sounds…

The merciless caresses of summer winds brought desire to the forefront. In trysts stolen in the afternoon in our homestead, we bathed in foreplays, and then reveled with slow dances, probing the slippery tourmaline transparency, nude.

Autumn falls, cold zephyrs, dry leaves swirling drew us out, to watch the maple baring itself, and we touched and smiled, and knew it was time, for yet again seeking kisses, a little wild, the champagne and wine, and nakedness by the fireplace...

Winter arrived with a white shroud, as we hibernated in the log cabin. There was absinthe and dreams. Snuggling closer, restless making love, making timelessness weaves and the warmth grew deep in our sleep, and we dreamed again.

When we woke, it was spring. The snow became water, and it was the little yellow flower enticing, entreating. It was hunger, and we kissed hard, and then, it began again, we ran in and undid clothes, and the bed welcomed our frenzy.

kanchan bhattacharya

The Moon was growing. From crescent to gibbous to fullness to hunger to foreplays, from darkness to twilight to bright.

The seasons found chance, reasons for ecstasy, and we lived life in timelessness forever...

She was the breeze that passed through my fingers, invisible, synchronized with mirages of wild lusty breasts, of hungry concave hollow hordes of carnivorous dreams, and yes, thoughts that sang in wordless forays into the mind through the ether between us.

I am the magician, caught in a word trap, alone on a sand dune, exiled by a disarrayed spell. I am sad, because all the magic I know does not work in this quantum space. I am thirsty, yet the oasis remains far away, it recedes into sunsets.

This is love on a page unknown, an open journey, no destination to reach. We are new here, growing into the chrysalis, a dream not yet formed.

We have chosen to be- I am, she is, but the planes of existence have not anchored yet. There is light, and there is the breeze. A little mad, a little of all that could be, but not quite that which I wish...

     kanchan bhattacharya

Space Time

A thought across space time, rain on a tin roof speaks in a monotonous voice, a rambling monologue. I think of those folded junctions, between her arm pit and breasts, between her breasts and beneath. Lust, when it happens and happens too often, is a crazed treacle, a crazed glistening set of lips, crystal specks, and a book lying face down, open at the bookmark as it sleeps abandoned in the middle of a tryst with sleep.

Raindrops, paper boats
Wet joys afloat, caresses
Tactile, tactless, lust

Rain sings. Rain brings deluges of many kinds. She asks if it was a cloud burst inside her and I laughed. It was a joy, the terminus of destinations sought in love, the roar of thunder, flashes of kisses, rhythms of tango.

Ceaseless rain, iambic
Intrusions seduce; high lows
Push, pull, tidal waves

And it rains, the resonant onomatopoeia of lust sounds, raindrops on a tin roof, an open book of poems, the cosmic poet in love with his muse.

*May I write words more naked than flesh, stronger than
bone, more resilient than sinew, sensitive than nerve*
~ Sappho

An ocean's roar
Fills all emptiness within
As I walk on sand

Wild stories begin this way.

Hallucinated, I keep two facets at the same time, between
the sober self, or the drunk poet, locked inside. There is
indeed a maelstrom of emotions inside me whereas on
the outside, I am calm, multitasking.

What can libido do, except provoke, and there are
moments I do not wish it to die. The mind of promiscuity,
every woman kisses differently, every breast has a differ-
ent kind of intoxication. How do I respond to that? You
have responded to this internally, and I have a story, or,
a poem to write.

It is a deluge- a stranger walks on intimate streets with
secrets behind brick walls, wounded words strung high
on signposts, like pigeons perched. A cold drawn out
shadow behind invisible sorrows haggles with street-
lights.

When I talk to you
I listen to your eyes; rain
Floods me, unawares

Graffiti waves, painted hands at thoughts that cross streets clutching petticoat hems in ankle deep rivers, wading slowly, unsure where the next foot would fall. It is a time, when unbidden came the roaring rain. It was night, wet streaks on windowpanes, and a gust of wind rushed in from the door that stayed ajar, witness.

Just images on high stiletto heels. Women of the night, mirages of the day. chance encounters with poets, dream words on papyrus rolls wash up on the strangest of shores. And salt still remains in eyes where love is lost, amid waves incessant, relentless, ardour with tsunamis and the volcanic rumbles, deep throated desire caught on seismic messages...

Sleep with unknown words
Woman; mistress of a night,
Of sultry lust, verse

Every bit that you see of me, the dust from the mines, the soot on my face, the yet to dry sweat becomes a decoy, steeped in honey. Inside lies the craving for the unknown, the woman in you.

As I sleep, my head rests on my arms. I feel the radiance of your body, faraway, hidden, yet with me.

I listen to the sounds of the night and hear the dew trampling the green things with wet kindness, the cold, and the low stir of replies as the wind blows.

I hide my elbows, woman. I have blood and bare skin, crawling too long. On my chest are furrows that you left. Still red, still hurting, and deep.

The night lulls me to sleep. I dream of a long gone by tomorrow. When we would be old, and in love.

I have walked you to the door, and it stays ajar. You may someday walk in, my gentle tornado!

      kanchan bhattacharya

Crescendo

My dream took me to the mountain of red mud, where one can climb into the sky or slide into bottomless ravines. I was with you walking up and up. I listen to you all the time. I found many abandoned homes along that arduous climb, but not a place I could call mine.

You led the way, and sometimes trailed far behind. You took my hand and hauled me up whenever I slipped. It was a dream alright, the sun never slept for a hundred days. We reached the crest line and walked into the void. It was bluer than the sea, and brighter than the sun.

Recall came with the tug of a woman's voice from a faraway past. Here you are, my love. Sunrise came in with a song. It took time to understand. It was a dream of death, and therefore I am.

Alive... a speck of paint on a cosmic canvas, a songbird with a strand of straw, painting the Universe... the owner of the sands of Time scripting Destiny...

A dream is a subliminal awakening, a parallel life in intangibility.

The Law of Darkness

As wants grow upon ether, shadows too grow longer and evenings progress into the night. In the alcove of secrets, we seek the light of what can be and call that destiny. Silence is dark, for those who have ceased to be for each other. The ether of existence has no waves, it is a tunnel carrying Time. And with these inveterate assertions, dreams are like butterflies, are my touches necrophilia reborn in my wantonness?

Perchance we came across and said magic things and sex was bountiful in midnight interchanges of bacchanal passages, insignificant distresses. A dawn person, tying petticoats strings of goodbyes and kisses; in the carpet layers of success, just her to taste?

Wants and wanton; Bohemian passion; this music of lips upon lips and mango in summer, hissing pythonesses predicting this mundane fall from heavens to the rudeness of failure.

There is a law. The Law of Darkness- an index finger tracking the cleaved truths of her breasts or the tactile nothings, muriatic acid of knowledge, she was, now lost in the bubbles of midnight baths, evanescent like camphor. This galaxy has its own inexorable rules- we are fragile; we finally find out Nirvana.

In noodles and chilies- I then ask you the – last query, you lay me to death?

      kanchan bhattacharya

A translucent candle flickers with warm molten tears,
shadows twist on distant walls.

The darkness finds its voice; a waterfall undresses;
verbs appear to walk and trek with kisses, dream breaks.
I memorize your skin, every fold that unfolds, every
dream that you bring lives in stories untold.

In a coterie of whispers, smiles sleep, a blanket shrouds
magic and with forlorn touches, pretense began.

The candle stares at darkness; black smoke merges with
all things we never said.

Pompei on fire; Atlanta slides into the sea; wuthering
winds, withering stones; night speaks; nearer home,
pigeons flutter their wings and destroy the remnants of a
dream interlaced with sleep.

It is a monologue; I still love you. The candle flame
radiates tangible incense in the moments before darkness
becomes all...

Confessional

Behind the window, he was prim and let me confess after I grabbed my lipstick tube, for that made things easier than when I am naked. I dip into my handbag and take out wiped out traces of mascara, wet wipes, innocent scraps of paper, and a testimonial from the Devil.

And I knew that He who sat behind the laced wooden grill in the cubicle was the man who groped me in the subway rush. He had the same perfume. But then, I wonder, all men wear it when they travel in the subway of favours.

I wonder about the darkness and the men behind the grill. The grill makes me feel secure about lust. He listens because there is nothing else to it. I would confess to sins that never visit me through the holes in the wall. I see His eyes. And I feel His palms you know where.

I feel awakened in a river boat with Hades. My confessions are like gunshots of adrenaline. I feel holy, this is a vantage point packaged and insulated in a didactic experience learning about myself. The confessional window is a subliminal purely intuited body, messed up.

I find the similes. Crossing the lines, that see through veil between two worlds of me and Him. I confess about his sins and mine. I paint my lips once again. We would meet after dinner.

A night that sleeps not- but whispers her charms in moonlit songs in zephyrs and gales; an ocean that gently touches its shores with ripples and asks questions with its tides; a little bird on my windowsill, chirping and reminding of that once upon a time; of snowflakes on my palms melting away my fever of longings.

Bring me a summer, a blazing bloom, red hillsides of rhododendrons- I wait on the steps of a porch, I slept for a century of moments in reminiscence. Your lips and your eyes, an image alive, swirling inside me, the thump, thump of heart beats, microcosms when the only word is a diphthong tied to mandolin, four strings strumming gently, and yes, elixir.

The last stars bid the morning goodbye. I place my fingertips on the alien. She stirs and begs me to pour on the promised caresses, kisses that taste like absinthe, begin the storm.

And then sunlight shone on torsos carved, moment to moment, in movements fluid, a ballet of joy. I have memorized your kisses...

Caresses asleep
Images stir a little
Love me. Love me not...

         kanchan bhattacharya

Impeachment

The descent from innocence into the valley of reality began on a summer day laced with heat and sweat; the twain, an old lover, and a yet to be mistress; and there were footsteps laid on dust, stone, and a steep slope.

They walked into the valley of tiny waterfalls; almost in silence; there would the slayer of conscience, man, and woman, looking for the forbidden fruit, yet unknown and Satan lurked.

Do not, the guide said, do not look back; this path is a mirage; seldom does one return unscathed. Once the nadir is reached, you may look up at the sun on the distant zenith. Bare yourself man, woman, and bathe.

The pool of Wisdom would begin the impeachment of innocence; your naked souls would be purged of all things but Knowledge…

Life is a long walk
Through a waterfall of Time
A skylight still dark

The Piano Woman

She paints herself in a mirror; the kohl around her eyes in the image behind the red oxide of mercury mellows, melts; in Time, she becomes a cloud. The years change her to rain and that rain seeps into me.

She is now a brown chocolate pomegranate. And all she is, is still infinite yet infinitesimal; she morphs into pirouetting verses of intense chroma, in waves ranging from pianissimo to fortissimo.

The mirror is in the eyes of a man in inversed role; the rouged silvered glass that hides all I have in my thoughts.

I am reading a book. Woman, in touches of fragrance and turning the strands of hair that become paper, pages, moist words, intimate caresses of an insatiable breeze.

When she plays the piano, I hear her soul in an arpeggio, her fingertips dancing in a serial cascade of black and white whispers.

I peruse the lines beneath the sketch; a woman is a ballet paused, a lyrical flight waiting for the passage of the signature andante of the introduction...

     kanchan bhattacharya

Eventide Sunset

When you begin a poem, you want to write of her ripe
lips; a wide abyss in terms of age had inhibited you- she
was born when you were twenty, and at your thirty-three,
she had bloomed.

And she ran away from eyes that sought her; where were
you then no one knew, nowhere near; she was in the
know of the myth called birds and bees and the stork.
She was lithe, nubile, a sprite, on fire.

Life became a wall of sheet glass, or a mirror; at your
forty, she found love and wed; you never knew her even
then, the mistress to be someday. She is now tired at the
mundane, and she is laden with ennui. She needs to be
elsewhere. With you.

And you needed a rebirth, unaware she lives next door.
Perchance, come the changes in your heart. She texts
you sometimes about her inner feelings; poems, pretexts
to seduction. Both- you at sixty, and she at forty have
seen it all. Like you, she too says, age is a number. And
this was destiny, a destination to be reached.

Her eyes are blue, and deep. The cloud lingers in her
coiffeur; you notice her fingers on the piano. Long and
manicured. She knows all about you too.

Perhaps a lover matching her desire, whenever. The
flight begins one day. You hold her hands in a car ride,
five hundred miles before it happens. It is déjà vu. She
overcomes it all and says yes to intimacy, trysts in a nest.

eros : unleashed

At first, she weeps, and you wipe away your tears. She withers at home. You, in yours.

You have that secret; you believe now that life so far was a lie, this is so late; magical and yes in delightful hidden guilt; you need to be dead together, to be born lovers, synchronized in contemporary compatibility. She too clings to you and says yes, it is time to go.

To sync with her. You leave together and eject the wounds of the lost twenty years and choose to pass into the new womb, and hope. Perhaps you can say; rebirth may not be a myth.

The inquest is brief. This was suicide, each at their own place. In love, talking on phone until death within minutes of each other, separated. Time stopped; the years escaped. The story morphs to the first person in each incarnation. Sweet, bitter, a walk on broken shards, a melody of hope, a death and Phoenix like lust. Heart break, and a breach of trust. Mists, fogs, lies.

Lovers find peace sometimes thus. Hello she says, tonight. You suggest a moonlight dinner on the Mayfair terrace, a home away from home, a hundred miles away. The storm begins again. Elsewhere.

Summer squalls; humid
Dark clouds; eventide amber
Straw nests, dust to dust...

          kanchan bhattacharya

Last Love

A thought arrives. Moonlight walk, dew, and winter, I sometimes go to the rooftop to touch the cold air. Sometimes you and I write texted poetry. We arrive at a labyrinth of duality. Us.

If my life is scaled to twenty-four hours, I am at my second twilight. Past sunset- you have become the last amber glimmer. Into my sleep, I light a cigarette, then two, then another absent mindedly.

Walking becomes a fall of footsteps. Rain. Dancing. Falling in love. Cavalcades of many things, a windfall?

Then...this weave of life...that too can't be, no words can describe the weave of life. Words play. I would love to weave myself, into the fabric around you, into Time.

I would love to be a droplet, slithering into your open palms. Where's this going, you ask; love-wards, I say, my beautiful woman, on an Odyssey through the seas of empathy, through memory in a fall, through Time's vortices, as midnight sits on my palm.

I cannot say I love you; I cannot say I can.

It is a stark place; white. Two beds in an ICU. Time makes sounds; pip, pip, pipping past the corridors. A nurse remains on a death watch, watching us.

A thought arrives; I ask to be turned to face your empty bed.

Silence tells stories, autumn skies hide tears of time; you whisper no more…

Clouds, darkening skies,
Silver lines, golden sunbeams
Images, imagine…

　　kanchan bhattacharya

Undead

Because love was not fiery enough, I imagined you were a piece of a porcelain sugar pot lined with arsenic and cinnamon, or, as an option, chosen with recklessness- a can of bewitched sulfides that came alive with a robot well versed in the arts of pleasures.

You often said I was a satyr running with the wind galloping impetuously, until you broke the rhythms. It is an echo that never fades, oh yes, oh yes. An image never erased, breasts over hungry lips all inside my head, inside the paranoiac stories that ricochet a million times in a white out space.

But you are safe because love is a disease, not fiery enough for arson inside my head, nor enough for you to trust with the snakes. Love is a synopsis, writhing, slithering in fluids, little floods and oozes that flow with fear and reach out for i-Pills after unsafe sex.

It is worth the fear. It is all inside my head in a heap of China, fungal growths, and nurses and sterile walls, a trolley, straps, pains, yells and shots of luminol, gatosils and soon to be that towel in my mouth, wires, and the tinkling electricity again, and again, until I sleep, undead...

Undone

Mineral cactai,
quicksilver lizards in the adobe walls,
the bird that punctures space,
thirst, tedium, clouds of dust,
impalpable epiphanies of wind.
The pines taught me to talk to myself.
In that garden I learnedto send myself off.
Later there were no gardens.

~ Octavio Paz
A Draft of Shadows
and Other Poems

Alone with Jacques Lacan

He is on a feud with Freud. Sigmund cries inside my mind all night, Jacques sings, he sounds nervous.

She and I huddle inside a shack. In a corner, there is a curled cat. Next to me is a blackboard, and a hurriedly scribble note. "Your future stands over the middle finger" it says. We grin and let that be. With a broom and a swab, we say abracadabra, we battle the cobwebs...

Lacan digs his nose. Freud speaks aloud, dreams do not necessarily tell who all you slept with. It is a pointer to old doors, and places to raid.

We kiss and look for curtains. We hunt for the old coir foam mattress and discover kittens and a python. Startled, the python climbs a window, and then, exits through the skylight. We find the four-poster beneath the mattress beneath the remnants of the cobwebs.

Freud sulks, feeling ignored. Lacan yells for a poet. Carl rises from the darkness, and says Sire, all the poets are dead in the century beyond my death.

We stand outside the cabin. We begin our lovemaking beneath the stars, after tossing a piece of white Phosphorus on the room.

Freud squeals with delight. Lacan walks out with a cigar; Carl plays the Moonlight Sonata.

We have arson. We burn too, we are on fire. A fire engine

arrives and spurts wanton gallons of liquids, and the cabin becomes dust.

We gather ourselves after the dream. The cinders are in bloom, a galaxy of rhododendrons. There is only one of us, alone all night in a cave.

Jacques Marie Émile Lacan was a French psychoanalyst and psychiatrist, described as "the most controversial psycho-analyst since Freud".

                    kanchan bhattacharya

Once, at 15, I decanted lust, I bathed too long, you know, how desire was then- it was not a trauma; as much as making love can be, without refractory gaps.

They may say I walked through a glass door, trying to choose between jouissance and the break away from a child's nascent libido caught in a turnstile.

Perhaps, trying to scale walls to break in and reach an uncertain mistress, a little older, eternal, external in an interlude of delusions, a bit poetical, embedded in echo mimetic onomatopoeia, in primary essence of things Lacan said were Real, symbolically, his 'a'.

I decanted lust, the slipperiness of soul.

Undo this rain, move your touches far away from my skin, but remain with your words in my ears, remain all over me, afloat, swim, insane...

Undo what I understood, begin with the clouds, the rolls of thunder, let your hair tumble with showers of fragrance, soft silence, trembling with unsaid promises, promiscuous, gratuitous, alien.

Undo my soul, bring me the night of Neverness that passes always in mountain high waves, the torn sails, broken masts with serpents speaking entwined, endurance lost in the swoop of a tornado, delusions walking and bringing the verse of Maya, mesmerizing

Leave me alone but remain, the throbs of forever sins re-awakened, the stories of adieus etched forever. Bring me the wine, change, break the rules that hold back the tremors of beginnings sans end.

Abandon me but bite me, make me the garden where you become the redwood spruce, implanted, timeless. Write me the primordial verse once again, take me to Elsewhere, the daydreams that tell me we shall never cease. Undo me, once again, I dare you Poet, ink your words, conjure lust, arson.

    kanchan bhattacharya

I plead, all night, typing messages on your nakedness, yet, you whispered "hush, your grammar is a mess, making love is never done, unless you hear my yes".

I ruffled her hair, and I smiled. Indeed, it was there in her eyes. Silver and golden streaks of hair rouged somewhere and tattoos of wet, the prints of failed tries.

I nestled deep, fragrance into my breathing invaded, tiptoeing and pirouetting in a ballet paced by heart sounds, a muted thunder, and cymbals slithering to magical rushes of winds, and in came the summer of delights...

Eros, said my Conscience, Eros lies all the time, Eve is asleep, and you must lay down too, into the abyss from where comes the spring of Amour. This death, the intermission, the red night and the canopy labelled exit.

And then came the script. The pages unfurled a story of a decade, the marks of passion, the trails of abrasion, the dancing until dawn and drunken words slurring again and again.

Rain, intruder, wild
Hail drumming on windowsills
Tender palms, her ayes

Un-Love: the verb of surprises and sorrow

Because un-loving is a poem walking away- it is easier to surrender, to seek love in the abyss where light interplays with black glitters, how do I un-belong? It was a permanence that permeated in every pore of us.

Love is a papyrus scroll- a kiss squeezes a little out. A palm on her back, and she presses her breasts into me. Elsewhere, there is synergy- un-belong, un-doing each other, to un-love? Love is that heat, molten as is a volcano's offerings of lava and pumice, pummeling and seeking crevices to fill. From near liaisons in real life- when affairs become tantalizing, we wind up. Un-loving is the wind that wears rocks. We have not found the knots to un-do. They were un-done and burnt...

Shall we un-love then, remove the kisses, and gently un-wind, help each other with kisses, and walk away, return the keys at the reception thirty floors below, to the marionette who smiles, and un-smirks, when we say, two beds, we are un-checking in, it is a time to un-arrive...

Is it love? Did un-plan yesterday when you said you love me?

We are un-checking in finally. Erasing time, but yes, un-goodbye!

     kanchan bhattacharya

Pawns in a game, in diagonals and rows of checkers, coffee cups and used spoons, and Braille messages, libido astir in otherwise a mess- castled and hemmed in, a few chairs, tabletops, upset maids, waitresses, their aprons imprinted with stains of wasted food, walking past.

And there is hunger. The order- a distant memory. I want to eat. Eat us. And you seem to know, we need an exodus. And I am thirsty, spelt L-U-S-T. The aroma of food permeates. I dream of food. I ask, shall we kiss?

I have moved us- I turn to face the kitchen door. The clientele has all moved a little and are staring at that door, quiet, lulled in the orgy of wait. The gleam in their eyes says it all… a kitchen on fire. I dream of the imaginary belt of bombs tied around my midriff.

I awoke to her screams. Here comes our order. And, no, it walks to the next table. In my heart is a wave of disappointment. I want to eat her.

The chaser arrives. The food will follow too! The t-buds begin to drool, and I sharpen my swords and fork. My canines and molars bite my tongue.

There comes the waiter… just the fifth of rye! Dinner is a light year away!

I have written three pieces of haiku on linen spread on the tabletop, a torrent of libido.

He sleeps with a Muse from the other side of acceptance; he has new poems each night; some speak of soul, some of conscience. No favors asked, he forges a bridge on a quiescent flow, there is no ebb, no neap, no high. Just ripples.

They wait; he in his eventide years, always lost in his den; she, now in her zenith, works somewhere, and she speaks to wide eyed young adults, and she worships no idol, be it known, just as he is a guy of no gods, atheist, a pagan, a fallen one.

They talk of all things, bonded in magic words; there is nothing to be said; and they own all the time, all things across a thin line, lined with barbed wires and hate.

The bridge is tenacious, never breaks. No way can they fall in love; the river is a flow on sands of illusions, allusions, metaphors, and tenderness.

Homes happen in strangers' hearts; one finds a poem, one finds a light; they share many a river of hope; they share a past, and they find a consonance amid sibilant whispers, that come hither in their rhythms, rhymes, blank verse.

Looking for a continuation...

kanchan bhattacharya

Tarot Cards

A bit of passing passion, the pair reach out.

He is wearing a shallow smile, bare chested in boxing shorts and gloves. In her, the eye of envy, and a rhythmic speaking in grunts, love-words, gifts of speeding hurts…

Imagine, lovers exchanging vows of fire with aimed volleys to maim, to end all resistance only to surrender in the climax, lying on the floor, a countdown before they take away the fallen one somewhere

To live, to love, kissing the image in the mirror, wearing the shroud of I don't care, I don't know if I am hurt. "Are you still here" is all they ask. The dream is over, morning speaks in a koel's voice, the breeze ignites other longings.

There are spillovers of mixed thoughts, you reach out to touch the unhappiness of a strange day, strangers in the streets and the many needs that never get over, stories told by tarot cards…

What remains there to ask for, if not solitude, if not the bliss of emptiness?

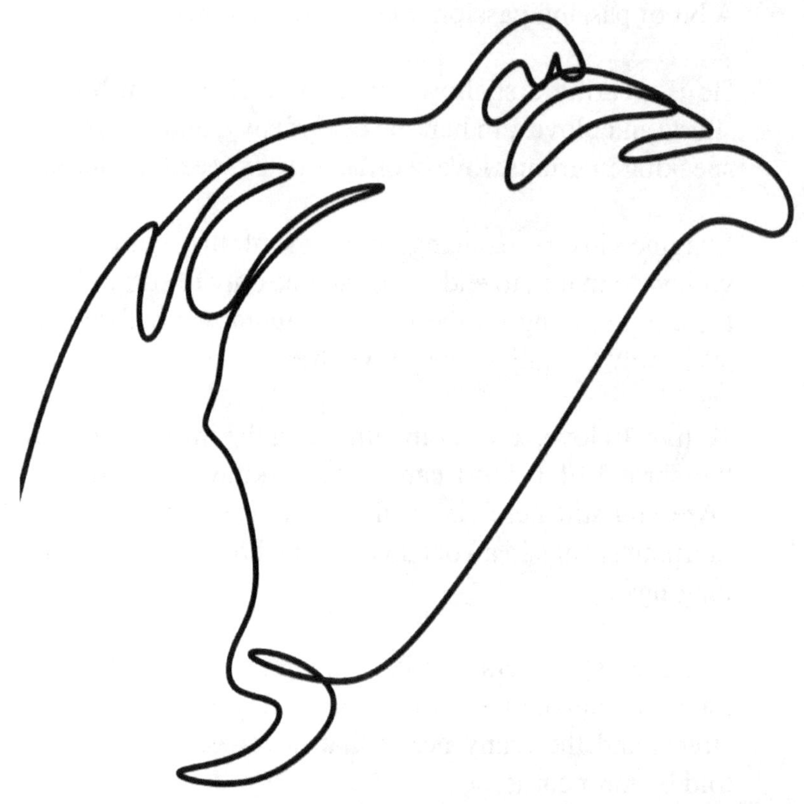

kanchan bhattacharya

The Web

Visualizing you, I began drawing an imaginary line, along your nose to lips, to your chin on this passage of love, a dream of touches, but I wanted to draw more, a mobius curve around your breasts.

We weave our dreams with errant fingers tracing paths for new discoveries. The line moves slowly past the chin, the neck, and pauses for soft consents, through a vibrant valley, beads of sweat, sounds of resonant, deep breathing. And then, on a flat plain, seeking Pandora's home, the stylus paints an oasis.

A hunter stands still, contemplating his quarry at the edge of a ravine.

Night stares through silence
A dark kohled duo; greed and needs
Whispered their kisses-

The final impulses of deep thoughts, clouds, curls. Monsoon gently brought s listless night, curled kisses, lingering on lips. A shadow in the night may sleep on the dew that dawn seeks and thoughts of rain astir in my mind.

The line waits forever, the web is us- you and I in this Inverness, poised.

They come at night, speak in alien voices, birds from a distant land. The din is unbearable, hordes of geese, predators with unimaginable grace, with wings of white.

The marsh falls midway. She wants me to awaken and stand by and shoot the birds at midnight. I squirm and pick up my camera and ask her to pretend she is the goose on my bed; and then I do the movie.

I open my eyes; she is gone; I am on my bed, the summer night is again astir in this city of concrete, asphalt lanes; there is no lake, the sound of geese is a mirage, the leaky tap dripping into a bucket. Water from Cauvery has arrived in the taps...

She mews aloud. Let me out, she says. I curse and step out. On the floor is an empty bottle of vodka, and a few paper bags that once held dinner.

Out- I tell the feline. She knows my mood! And then I look at the mess. It has been days since I did my bed. I look at my chest. The girl I remember had a name, a body of lust, and she liked to please. At forty plus, a treasure with beautiful large breasts and a flat belly.

I turn on the lights; she has left her mark on the mirror, a kiss in chocolate shades and a number, ten digits; a message that said, you sleep beautifully, and the love making is a soft melody. Call me.

The last thing she said was she wants to be like a Siberian crane in flight.

The silent street lies thirty stories below, and at minus two degrees on the horizon is a crimson dawn. Clouds in black change colors. I ask for a cup of tea, Room Service says, let me sleep, wait till seven am.

Ok, Google, next page.

The DNA of metaphorical dreams lie on my bed with the wrinkled linen. Chameleon like, they change color, monsoon chases the clouds, sometimes though I return for the ritual of kisses memorized...

Merciless summer- a wanton sweltering breeze strokes my wounds again. I close my eyes in the shower; I imagine the rain, and sing- raindrops keep falling on my head... The reverie has begun.

Ok Google. New page...

Dusk Again

My instincts play hard. I am curious, as insidious as alcohol- I slip my words into you- whispering. "I say", I say- "your slippers are dainty"! What have you brought to me- the darkness here was always mine, now your cold hands probe me, seeking my eyes, blind as I can be, in a stupor of wine, perhaps?

I may ask, whatever in the end you may seek, gooseflesh and tremors that stray. Perhaps you would ask again, in the contralto of the night, permeating like racing nails, blood trails that may in the morning die- no, ask me nothing, the answers you already know!

But ask, my past on record, my sins with you yet to begin in forethought awash, destined surely- but for the will to walk beyond, lost in synesthesia, in the din the chalked lines, the bounds never torn. I wait, you pine, the forecast of imperious moods ahead, we wait for the sails to fill, the first step, tender, diffident impious, modesty shorn.

What have I brought to you? May be neither I, nor you would answer, but we ask whichever is the way, in this dusk?

I see the shimmering mirage, poetry in your eyes, poetry on your lips, memories sparkle in snowflakes, eddying, beckoning!

It is dusk again!

 kanchan bhattacharya

Dionysus

It was not destined to be.

He had the deep voice, and the charm of Dionysus and he knew everything- he was ancient.

She had the smile of the moon, the grace of a gazelle, a poet, of that prime age when time stood still.

They often wondered what brought them together.

At 40, I was not getting any younger. He was always around, with an inexplicable air of detachment around himself. I was sure he was in love with me, but never spoke of it. I admired him, but never knew I was in love with him.

I had a broken life once. He was living in one, an incomplete marriage. I suspected he was old, but virile. He perhaps made love like a Greek god, or was he the Satyr, Insatiable One.

And he was a reckless one.

I always suspected he guarded his past so well, never told me much about his life. Was he an imposter?

~ Dionysus is a Greek God who represented many aspects of human experience, including wine, life, death, theatre, and fertility

Your, those toxic lips/bound in shades of rouge/layers of cosmetics.

Sometimes I feel I would spread eagle you/on the table a taxidermist filling each port with indiscretions and arsenic. I have called Euphoria/waiting for that arousal/of hurricanes/with whispers. Soft, candid virulent volcanic/ trials, iterations/lips, intoxicated rouged, toxic un-lovers, poets manic.

Nothing but an accident; the collusion of bodies in Mid-night's lanes. Some whispers, some coffee stains, some froth, memorized once again.

I have this intimate and intricate relationship with verse; poems often revel, we find homes, in the weightlessness of themes of my Id, my trysts with the limbs of Venus.

Bubbles rise in a marsh, a gaggle of geese walking in cacophony, and vowels, diphthongs on webbed feet, wings stretched, a skein in white.

Life is a long lease rain forest; smiles you lease; as a lessor, someone plants little noisy greed words like

touch me not-
drooping leaves
bow deep…

 kanchan bhattacharya

Edible, partly carnivore, I straddle the heaps, the grave of Venus, like a locust on fiery loins intemperate, seeking violent reunions.

Partly carnivore, I ask her "Eat me too!" I offer her a meal of Life, a union wrapped in the cosmetics of erotica, a garden of apples and flesh, edible even when alive in this garden of the glowing candles.

Partly Jurassic, I clamor for feed of human flesh, intemperate at midnight, when food meets the mouth of kisses and bloodied teeth, incisions, serrated, cleaved orifices and hissing snakes of intimate breath oozing life, strident, vibrant hips, yes, her eyes and soul.

In part, and then, in entirety, I swallow her, as she throbs over me, sensual until Eternity arrives.

     kanchan bhattacharya

Dopamine

Two minds on cravings - one says wanton things, other asleep in deep body-speak. Every piece a calligraphic Eros, like Nabokov, psychotic, yet inviting, the first thought she arouses with her words, an image of a girl, her tangerine breasts, small, prime, lustrous, sunlit...

The first snowfall at midnight, the moon coming alive, man to woman face to face and knowing the depths of their being together like fireflies know the forest, luminescent even in darkness, waiting for the happenings of tides.

Sitting against a black curtain, he speaks of enchantment in her eyes, dopamine messages seeking to explore her torso, seeking caresses of joy, the beginning of a wildfire.

She stands and stretches, a lithe feline form. He watches the messages from Venus, that oestrogen stimulus. She stands, silhouetted, the spotlight on her face. She says stand and touch, propose what you want. Speak your verse, mediate with tactile thought, in serotonin spreads on my skin.

Body speaking lust
Arousals in her areoles
In audience his eyes

They read anyway; two poems done together. Calliope smiles between the rejoinders in a new world of twilight. I can type my dirty thoughts in unknown fonts on pristine white virtue; incoherent, rhyme-less sentences, prose poems plead softly with arrhythmia.

I can sing.

Nabokov : a Russian-American novelist, poet, translator, and entomologist, born in Imperial Russia in 1899.

Calliope : In Greek mythology, Calliope is the Muse who presides over eloquence and epic poetry; so called from the ecstatic harmony of her voice.

                    kanchan bhattacharya

I need a body in your world. I remain maimed in mine, asleep on a liquid nitrogen bed.

Poignant, puissant, yes because the mind says no. No because matter is still matter, now is here. We are here, but absent, I still am. You still are the woman.

Now is here, this time to leave the quantum space of niches lost. Matter hits antimatter, three neutrinos and a quark, a little smoke and dust. A puff of beta, and gamma rays that say write, writhe, die, writ...

Odysseys begin again. I cannot let go a cab ride to Mainland China. You have hijacked my thoughts, shanghaied my soul.

I still think of matter, antimatter, and elves.

I have begun; the unwinding of Time, the escape movement of a spring in a mechanical clock, the body writhes in pain.

Yet memories return naked; some speak in husky undertones and provoke for a once again. Some just stand and tell, it can never be enough, this knowing of all we could do to ourselves in abandoned places.

And the Mind; what of it that remembers yours, singing in the little red car, yet crying inside as we said good bye once again, unsure if this was not the edge of darkness, of the precipice, falling apart, taking a chance...

Once upon a time; happenstance happened. Then it wound itself too tight and slipped away downhill.

Whispering wanton Time never returns. Images astir at 3 am in dark, rain caresses the walls, and lanterns sway in resonance. I am still. I wait, because there is never to be the need of anything hereafter in this once forever death...

Rain, now your absence
Tells stories, unknown affairs
That hold wet sighs, sobs...

Lovers

The blushing Eve and I are debutantes in this ancient art, sleeping along the path of exploration of our bodies and soul, Arctic and Antarctic zones of Eros. We are the caves, and we are the stalagmites and stalactites trying to tryst with tongues of frozen Times, and the standstill zephyrs created by the enchanted breathing of Hades and Persephone.

Love is a softness embedded in the improbability of chances. We found each other when we were not to meet. We meet and we wish it to happen, curtains falling on the past and footlights dimming to whispered asides, the baritones meeting sopranos amid the echoes and shadows that tell us to change the past and to choose a new script of destiny and destinations.

The woman holding my palm, and I are a pool of molten metal, a mercurial flow seeking a new home, a slow dance, a flickering flame, a breeze riding the tympanic hands of the Cosmos, the dream that pauses.

We are the Oneness of Chances. We are the mystery of forlornness meeting bliss, the harmony of Yin meeting Yang, a mono act play that begins and never ends.

And we are the heartbreak of all who loved us as we walk away from the past, shipwrecked mariners on new shores of caresses and kisses, a storyboard and a mural of waves, naked, clasped, a new world, surging tide, a tsunami into eternity.

Dawn, until darkness
Paints, woman, me, wanton wants
An August night ends

                    kanchan bhattacharya

Verse of Eros

Midnight hues framed in mahogany hang on the stark white walls in a room; lonely, stifled thoughts wait for a poem paused in silent voids in a faraway night.

Stillness braided with dark whispers speaks with skin to skin contact. Unbridled electric thoughts, preludes to more delights awaken. Upon trails of intense wants, the id plays mindlessly with naked torsos.

Myriad strings come to life in black mirrors, murmuring with vapour and serpentine caresses. Trespass is moments away. Her honeyed areolas beckon his admiring tongue...

I need your planet, he says. She unfolds her coiled body. Puissant surges begin the recital of the Verse of Eros.

Many thoughts scattered fluttering wishes, melodic alienation knocked down with kisses staring at nocturnal arias in this titanic limbo, the waves, erotic images, the naked Calypso

Calypso, in Greek mythology, the daughter of the Titan Atlas (or Oceanus or Nereus), a nymph of the mythical island of Ogygia.

Carnal in winter, distanced in dreams, a small rippling creek whispers gently- here is the sea, set sail-

Now the question you ask- can I lock the world in a few words? I say yes, my world would be you in my arms.

Can I paint it azure and turquoise, you ask softly. I say yes, you do remember my kisses, I remember your eyes...

    kanchan bhattacharya